D1068814

Conceived and edited by Solomon M. Skolnick
Designed by Lesley Ehlers

All photographs licensed by the Image Bank®
Photographs are, in order of appearance, by:

Pete Turner, Harald Sund, Kaz Mori, David Sharrock, Pete Turner,
Peter Hince, Joe Devenney, T. Chinami, Grant V. Faint,
David De Lossy, Michael Melford, Steve Satushek, Joanna McCarthy,
Miao Want, Michael Melford, Steve Satushek, Andre Gallant,
Stephen Wilkes, Alan Becker, Terje Rakke, Tomek Sikora,
Paul McCormick, Pete Turner, David De Lossy,
Harald Sund, Robert Farber, Kaz Mori

Afterword copyright © 1999
Peter Pauper Press, Inc.
202 Mamaroneck Avenue
White Plains, NY 10601
ISBN 0-88088-880-0
Printed in China
9 8 7 6 5 4 3

Visit us at www.peterpauper.com

Amazing Grace

THE BELOVED SONG

Amazing grace! How sweet the sound

That saved a wretch like me!

I once was lost but now am found;

Was blind, but now I see.

'Twas grace that taught my heart to fear,

And grace my fears relieved;

How precious did that grace appear

The hour(s) I first believed.

Through many dangers, toils, and snares,

I have already come;

'Tis grace hath brought me safe thus far,

And grace will lead me home.

The Lord has promised good to me,

His Word my hope secures;

He will my shield and portion be,

As long as life endures.

Yea, when this flesh and heart shall fail,

And mortal life shall cease,

I shall possess, within the vail,

A life of joy and peace.

The world shall soon dissolve to snow,

The sun refuse to shine;

But God, who called me here below,

Shall be forever mine.

When we've been here ten thousand years,

Bright shining as the sun,

We've no less days to sing God's praise

Than when we'd first begun.

Amazing Grace

was written by John Newton, an 18th century
sailor who spent much of his time at sea
as a slave trader. Newton, saved by Providence
from a cataclysmic storm, repented his sins
and became a minister.

Amazing Grace, the song, has made a transcendent
journey to the hearts and lips of believers through
two centuries, much as its inspired author made
a transcendent journey from his own heart
of darkness to God's light.